D1716595

# SWAT Teams

BY KIRSTEN W. LARSON

amicus
high interest

Amicus High Interest is an imprint of Amicus
P.O. Box 1329, Mankato, MN 56002
www.amicuspublishing.us

Library of Congress Cataloging-in-Publication Data
Names: Larson, Kirsten W., author.
Title: SWAT teams / by Kirsten W. Larson.
Description: Mankato, MN : Amicus, [2016] | Series: Protecting
    our people | Audience: K to Grade 3._ | Includes index.
Identifiers: LCCN 2015033740 (print) | LCCN 2015046771
    (ebook) | ISBN 9781607539858 (library binding) | ISBN
    9781681510255 (ebook) | ISBN 9781681510255 (pdf)
Subjects: LCSH: Police–Special weapons and tactics units—
    Juvenile literature.
Classification: LCC HV8080.S64 L37 2016 (print) | LCC
    HV8080.S64 (ebook) | DDC 363.2/3 dc23
LC record available at http://lccn.loc.gov/2015033740

Editor: Wendy Dieker
Series Designer: Kathleen Petelinsek
Book Designer: Heather Dreisbach
Photo Researchers: Rebecca Bernin and Aubrey Harper

Photo Credits: MILpictures by Tom Weber/Getty cover; Irfan
Khan/Getty 5; Andy Katz/Demotix/Corbis 6; Joe Amon/
Getty 9; matthrono/Flickr 10-11; SPUTNIK/Alamy 13; Irfan
Khan/Getty 14; Greg Smith/Corbis 17; Kayana Szymczak/
Getty 18; U.S. Navy photo by Photographer Mate 2nd Class
Jim Watson/Flickr 21; STEPHEN LAM/Reuters/Corbis 22-23;
Warships/Alamy 25; BenDC/iStock 26; Mikael Karlsson/
Alamy 29

Printed in the United States of America.

10 9 8 7 6 5 4 3 2 1

The author thanks Los Angeles Police Department's Lt. Ruben
Lopez for his assistance.

# Table of Contents

A Car Chase ................................ 4

A Day in the Life ......................... 8

Learning the Ropes ..................... 16

Working with Others ................... 24

Protecting Our People ................ 28

Glossary ..................................... 30

Read More .................................. 31

Websites ..................................... 31

Index .......................................... 32

# A Car Chase

A car speeds through the Los Angeles streets. The driver weaves all over the road. Police try to pull over the car. The driver speeds onto the freeway. Then his passenger shoots his gun at the police. Bang! Bang! Crash! The two men run from the car. They shoot some more! The police need help. They call in the SWAT team.

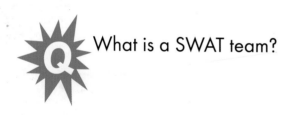 What is a SWAT team?

A SWAT team is called in for very dangerous jobs. They have the best training and the right gear.

 SWAT stands for Special Weapons and **Tactics**. Teams use military-like methods and high-powered weapons.

SWAT teams use dogs to help
search for bad guys. Dogs can
smell things better than people can.

The SWAT team arrives. They will help hunt for the bad guys. The team brings their dogs to sniff out the **suspects**. They find one man hiding behind a dumpster. He gives up and goes to jail. When they find the second bad guy, he shoots. The SWAT team takes him down.

# A Day in the Life

SWAT teams are a police department's special forces. They help in **high-risk** situations. Maybe a crook has a gun and refuses to give up. The SWAT team is called in. SWAT teams also rescue **hostages**.

To do their job, SWAT teams need special gear. They wear helmets and have goggles to protect their eyes. They also wear bulletproof vests.

 What kind of guns do they have?

Special gear helps protect a SWAT officer when he gets called into a dangerous mission.

Big ones. They may use automatic weapons. Some use sniper rifles.

About 12 SWAT officers respond to a call. Part of the team sets up a **perimeter** around the crime scene. They tell people in the area to leave. They make sure the bad guys don't leave.

SWAT **snipers** find a high place to set up. They get ready to shoot from far away if needed. They work as lookouts too.

Every member of the SWAT team has a job to do on the scene.

Some SWAT members are **negotiators**. They talk to the crooks. They try to get the crooks to give up peacefully. Most SWAT calls end without shots fired. If talks do not work, the team jumps into action. Using ropes, they scale tall buildings. They break down doors with battering rams. Crash! They free hostages and get the bad guys.

SWAT teams are trained to catch the bad guys and bring them safely out.

These officers make a plan.
They are searching for a person
who may have done a crime.

 Do all towns have SWAT teams?

In some places, a SWAT officer is a full-time job. In smaller police departments, officers may serve on the team part time. Other times, they patrol the streets. Or they might work as detectives.

In big cities, teams get called every day. Afternoons and nights are busiest. Teams in small towns may only get one call a month.

 No. Sometimes towns share a regional team.

# Learning the Ropes

Joining the SWAT team is hard.
Only experienced officers can apply.
Recruits need one to five years of police
experience.

Recruits must pass a fitness test. This
includes timed runs, push-ups, sit-ups, and
pull-ups. They complete obstacle courses.
They scale walls using ropes. They crawl
under barbed wire and pull heavy logs.
Only the best pass the test.

Team members hone their shooting skills at the gun range.

People may try to get into a
crime scene. SWAT officers
learn how to keep them safe.

 Can women work on SWAT teams?

SWAT members have to keep cool when there is danger. To test this, SWAT teams grill recruits in face-to-face interviews. They also talk to the recruit's bosses and people they work with. Does this person have what it takes?

After all the tests, the top people go to SWAT school. SWAT school may last a few months or just a few weeks.

Yes! SWAT teams hire the best of the best law enforcers.

During training, officers practice situations they will find on the job. Actors pretend to be crooks. They work to frustrate the officers. The officers must keep their cool. They must work together. Trainers watch the whole time. Who will be good enough to be on a SWAT team?

 Do teams use real guns in training?

Some trainees pretend to be criminals. New officers learn how to handle the bad guys.

Some do! The training houses have rubber walls. These walls soak up the bullets.

Passing SWAT school is not enough. Team members must keep training. They must pass fitness tests each year. On big squads, team members may work out for an hour each day. They must keep fit.

Many teams do drills with units from around the world. Urban Shield is a yearly drill. Teams face 35 different situations in 48 hours.

SWAT officers keep training so they are always ready.

# Working with Others

SWAT teams often work with **first responders**. When someone makes a 911 call, police, fire fighters, and emergency workers rush to the scene. They check out the problem. If necessary, they call the SWAT team.

**EMTs** may respond with the SWAT team. These people are medical experts. They stand by in case someone gets hurt.

EMTs help SWAT teams.
They take action if anyone
on the scene gets hurt.

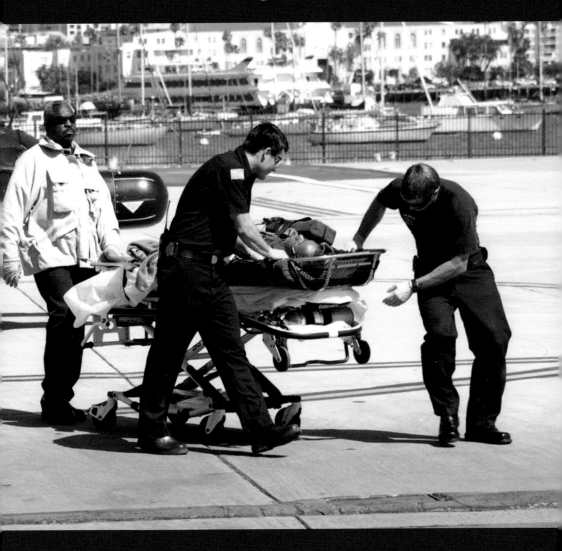

These workers wear protective clothes when they help SWAT teams deal with dangerous items.

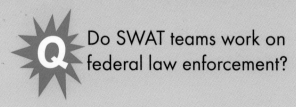

Q Do SWAT teams work on federal law enforcement?

SWAT teams often work with other police units. If a suspect has a bomb, the team calls in the bomb squad. The squad has dogs to find hidden bombs. The officers disable the bombs. Whew!

Sometimes SWAT teams find dangerous chemicals. Then they call the **hazmat team**. The team takes samples. They identify the chemicals and clean them up.

Yes, they do. The FBI and NASA have SWAT teams. Even the National Park Service has a SWAT team.

# Protecting Our People

Serving on a SWAT team can be very dangerous. Yet, if a bad guy says he will hurt himself or someone else, the team steps in. Most of the time suspects give up. But if they do not, the SWAT team is ready. They have special training and gear to get the job done. Hands up!

When a mission is very
dangerous, the SWAT
team is called in.

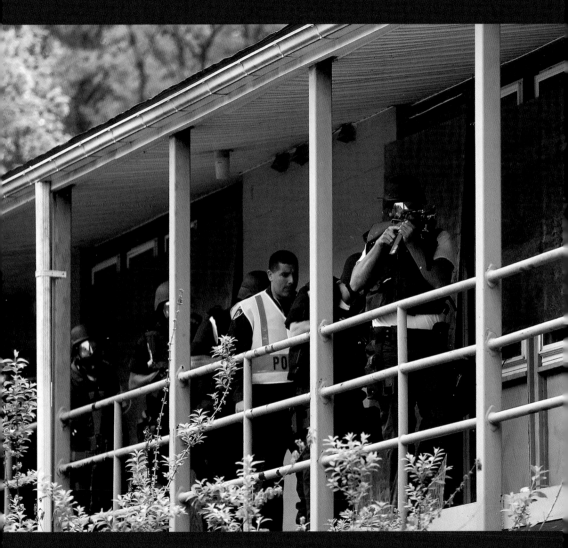

# Glossary

**EMTs** Short for emergency medical technicians; they help when people are hurt.

**first responder** A person like a firefighter, police officer, or paramedic whose job is to get to an emergency first.

**hazmat** Short for hazardous materials; hazmat teams are experts in dangerous things.

**high-risk** Likely to be harmful or dangerous.

**hostage** A person held against their will by a person demanding something like money.

**negotiator** A person who talks to others to come to an agreement.

**perimeter** A boundary around an area.

**sniper** A person who shoots very well from a long distance.

**suspect** Someone thought to have done something wrong.

**tactics** Actions and plans to get a job done.

# Read More

Grene, Tom. *SWAT: Special Weapons and Tactics.* Vero Beach, Fla.: Rourke Educational Media, 2015.

Ollhoff, Jim. *SWAT.* Minneapolis: ABDO Pub. Co., 2013.

Perish, Patrick. *SWAT Team Member.* Minneapolis: Bellwether Media, Inc., 2015.

# Websites

**FBI SWAT Tools of the Trade**
*http://www.fbi.gov/about-us/capabilities/fbi-swat-graphic*

**History of SWAT**
*http://www.lapdonline.org/metropolitan_division/content_basic_view/849*

**LAPD I Want to Know**
*http://www.lapdonline.org/i_want_to_know*

Every effort has been made to ensure that these websites are appropriate for children. However, because of the nature of the Internet, it is impossible to guarantee that these sites will remain active indefinitely or that their contents will not be altered.

# Index

bomb squads 27
dogs 7, 27
EMTs 24
FBI 27
first responders 24
fitness 16, 23
gear 8, 28
hazmat teams 27
hostages 8, 12
locations 15
Los Angeles 4
NASA 27

National Park Service 27
negotiators 12
police 4, 8, 15, 16, 24 27
recruits 16, 19
snipers 9, 11
SWAT school 19, 23
training 16, 19, 20, 21, 23, 28
Urban Shield 23
weapons 4, 5, 8, 9, 20, 21

# About the Author

Kirsten W. Larson has written dozens of books and articles for young people. She's proud to live near Los Angeles, California, home to the country's first SWAT team. Visit her website at www.kirsten-w-larson.com.